Summertime in the Forest

EDWARD ALAN KURTZ

Print • eBook • Audiobook

Copyright © 2016 Edward Alan Kurtz
Published by Stergiou Limited
All rights reserved.

Copyright
Summertime in the Forest
2016 © Edward Alan Kurtz
Images & Illustrations: Dreamstime Photo Stock
Cover image: © Tigatelu | Dreamstime.com
Back cover image: © Pflpitation | Dreamstime.com

Available in print, eBook and audiobook

ISBN: 978-1-910370-77-3 (Stergiou Limited-Assigned)
ISBN: 978-1-530762-04-0 (CreateSpace-Assigned)
ePub ISBN: 978-1-910370-63-6 (Stergiou Limited-Assigned)

Published by Stergiou Limited
Suite A, 6 Honduras Street,
London EC1Y 0TH, United Kingdom
Email: admin@stergioultd.com
Web: http://stergioultd.com
All rights reserved

CONTENTS

Chapter One	At Home in the Pine Tree	5
Chapter Two	The Backpack	11
Chapter Three	Making a Plan	19
Chapter Four	The Map	25
Chapter Five	Ready, Set, Go!	33
Chapter Six	Escape from Ridley's Ridge	39
Chapter Seven	Raging River	45
Chapter Eight	The Cave	51
Chapter Nine	The Second Cave	57
Chapter Ten	Mount Evergreen!	63

CHAPTER ONE

At Home in the Pine Tree

Once upon a time, there was a very special forest full of beautiful trees and other plants. Of course, there were other things in the forest. There were hills and mountains; there were valleys; there were several rivers; and there was a small lake that had been made when some beavers made a dam for their houses on one of the rivers.

The forest was also the home of many animals. In addition to the beavers, there were chipmunks, squirrels, otters, minks, deer, foxes, and many different kinds of birds. There were even some snakes, but they usually stayed to themselves and did not bother the other animals.

All of the animals knew each other and, for the most part, they were friends. Some of the animals were friendlier than others, but they all got along fairly well.

Of all of the plants in the forest, the most special one was the pine tree in the middle of the forest. It was the biggest and the oldest tree in the forest and all of the animals loved this beautiful giant old pine tree.

Some of the trees in the forest lost their leaves over the winter: but the old pine tree did not lose its leaves. It was an evergreen tree with needles. There were many other evergreen trees in the forest, but this old pine tree was the biggest and everyone in the forest knew about it.

It dropped some of its needles on the floor of the forest below, and this made a big soft area where the animals of the forest often went to rest or take a nap. It was also a good place to hold a meeting if there was something going on in the forest that the animals needed to talk about.

This soft area was especially good on a hot summer day. Spring was over now: all of the blossoms had dropped off the trees and other plants and the forest was thick with leaves.

Today it was a hot day in the forest, so there were several animals enjoying the

Image: © Liusa | Dreamstime.com

shade and the soft needles under the old pine tree. They heard some noises high up in the tree, but the noises didn't bother the animals: they knew who was up there!

The old pine tree was a place to rest and a place to have a meeting, but it was also the home of several of the forest animals. And this was where the noise was coming from.

At the top of the old pine tree were the homes of three birds and a squirrel. The three birds lived very close to the top of the tree and the squirrel lived a couple of branches below the birds.

The three birds and the squirrel were best friends. They lived so close to each other, and they talked to each other just about every day and had afternoon tea together almost every day. Who were these animals?

The three birds' names were Wendy the Warbler, Wally the Woodlark, and William the Woodpecker. And Sebastian the Squirrel lived just below them.

Each of these animals was unique and special, and each house was unique as well. Wendy was a very smart warbler. All the animals in the forest knew Wendy: she was kind and if anyone needed help, they could go to her for help. Whatever they needed, Wendy could help.

Each of these four animals had a favourite colour. Wendy's favourite colour was pink. Her front door was painted pink and inside of her house, just about everything you could think of was pink: her furniture, her bedspread, her walls, her rugs, her curtains. Even her teapot and teacups were decorated with pretty little pink roses.

While Wendy was known for being smart, her neighbour, Wally the Woodlark, was known for being very disorganized and very forgetful. He was a good friend, but he was often late for appointments or sometimes he just altogether forgot them! So when the other forest animals invited Wally to do something, they were never sure if he was going to show up or not.

Wally's house was on the other side of the tree from Wendy's house. His favourite colour was blue so his front door was coloured blue. And when he opened his front door and you peeped in you noticed two things.

The first thing you noticed was that just about everything was blue. And the second thing you noticed was that everything was in such a mess! Wally's rugs were blue, his furniture, his walls, his quilt, his slippers, and even his backpack was blue. They each took turns having afternoon tea, so Wally had a blue teapot and matching blue teacups.

And then there was William the Woodpecker. He was known for having a lot of energy and for always being busy doing this or that. He never sat still and he loved to be outside playing sports.

There was one very important difference between William's house and his friends' houses. William was a woodpecker and he had pecked a space inside the trunk near the top of the old pine tree that was big enough to make his house. After he was finished pecking, he added a door to the small hole that was just big enough for him and his friends to go inside.

He painted his front door purple because this was William's favourite colour. And inside his house there were lots of purple things like his walls, his furniture, a purple table cloth on his kitchen table, and a purple lampshade on the purple lamp next to his comfortable purple chair.

"I can't imagine where Sebastian is," said Wendy. "He's never late for tea."

The three birds, Wendy, Wally, and William, were sitting in Wendy's house enjoying their afternoon tea. Even Wally was there: he had been a little late, but not as late as usual.

Just then the three birds heard a very loud noise outside!

Image: © Vadmary | Dreamstime.com

CHAPTER TWO

The Backpack

The three birds ran to the windows at the front of Wendy's house. It was Sebastian the Squirrel! He was on his back on the branch outside of Wendy's house! The three birds opened the front door of Wendy's house. They looked at Sebastian and started to laugh.

He was wearing his new backpack and it was too heavy. So just as he was about to knock at Wendy's front door, he tipped over backwards and landed on his back. He wasn't hurt and so the four of them laughed as the three birds helped to take his backpack off. Now he could stand up.

Sebastian lived just below the three birds and their houses. While Wendy was known for being smart, and Wally was known for being disorganized, and William was known for being very active, Sebastian was known for being nosy. He loved to listen in on conversations, and he loved to spread gossip.

William had helped Sebastian build his house. He had pecked a hole in the trunk of the old pine tree a couple of branches below where the birds lived. It had to be bigger than William's house because Sebastian was bigger than William. And the hole where they put up the front door had to be big enough for Sebastian to go in and out.

Sebastian's front door was painted gray: this was his favourite colour and was also the colour of his fur. Inside of his house, there were many gray things, like his halls, his rugs, his bed, his kitchen table and chairs, and lots more.

But the most important thing in his house was Sebastian's gray coloured telephone. His telephone sat on a gray table next to a comfortable gray chair, because this is where Sebastian spent most of his time: on the telephone, gossiping!

And today he was wearing his new gray backpack.

"Why is this so heavy?" asked Wally.

"What ever have you put inside this?" asked Wendy.

Sebastian was a little out of breath because of carrying the heavy backpack from his house up to Wendy's front door.

He couldn't answer at first. "Come inside," said Wendy. "The three of us will carry your backpack inside for you."

Sebastian nodded his head as he panted and walked into Wendy's house. At the same time the three birds were having a hard time dragging the backpack into Wendy's house, but they finally got it inside the door.

"What is in that?" asked William.

Sebastian was sitting on a chair at the table where the birds were having their afternoon tea. He was still panting.

"Would you like a cup of tea?" asked Wendy.

Sebastian nodded, so she poured him a cup of tea and sat it down in front of him.

Finally he caught his breath: "Camping equipment."

The three birds looked at each other: they were surprised and confused.

"Camping equipment?" asked William.

Sebastian finished a sip of tea and then answered, "Yes. Camping equipment."

"Well, this is kind of a surprise," said Wendy. "What do you think of all this, Wally?"

As usual, Wally wasn't paying attention. He had helped the two other birds bring Sebastian's new gray backpack, but after they had all settled down inside of Wendy's house, Wally's mind had started to drift: he was thinking about washing his bed quilt since it was a breezy day.

Image: © Wongsalam77 | Dreamstime.com

"Wally?" asked Wendy. "Are you with us?"

"Oh, yes," answered Wally. "That new backpack is a wonderful shade of gray: it's just perfect for you, Sebastian."

They all groaned. "We were talking about camping equipment!" said Wendy.

"Oh," answered Wally. "Who's going camping?"

"Weren't you listening?" asked William. "We asked Sebastian why his backpack is so heavy. He said it was because of camping equipment."

"Oh, right," said Wally. "So who's going camping?"

Wendy and William and Sebastian all rolled their eyes, but continued with their conversation.

"Last night when I was in bed, just before I fell asleep, I had this brilliant idea," said Sebastian.

They all waited for him to explain.

"It's summertime, right?" he asked them.

They all nodded, even Wally who had forgotten about his quilt and was now thinking about the conversation.

"And what does everybody do in the summertime?" asked Sebastian.

"Try to keep cool?" asked Wally.

"No!" said Sebastian. "Go camping!"

"Camping?" asked Wendy. "Not everybody goes camping in the summertime?"

"You know what I mean," said Sebastian. "Maybe not 'everybody,' but a lot of people go camping."

"Why?" asked Wally.

"Why, what?" asked Sebastian.

"Why do a lot of people go camping?" asked Wally.

"Because!" said Sebastian. "It's fun and there's so much to see."

William was the active one among the friends, so he started to become very interested in this idea.

"I think you're right," he said to Sebastian. "The forest is huge and we've seen a lot of it, but there are places where we haven't been yet."

"Yes," added Wendy. "There is that tall mountain a couple of valleys from here that we can see from up here high in the pine tree. There might be all kinds of things to see."

"So what do you say?" asked Sebastian. "Do you want to go camping?"

"Yes!" answered Wendy.

"Yes!" answered William.

They all waited for the third "Yes!" but there was silence. Wally was staring out of the window: there was an insect sitting on a leaf just outside of Wendy's house.

"Wally!" said Wendy.

"Yes?" answered Wally.

"Camping?" asked Wendy.

"What about it?" asked Wally.

"We're talking about going on a camping trip," answered Wendy. "Would you like to go with us?"

"Oh, yes," answered Wally. "That could be fun. You know there's that really tall mountain a couple of valleys from here."

"Yes," said William. "That's where we're going."

Wendy had an idea: "We all have own backpacks. So why don't we each take some of your camping equipment out of your heavy backpack, Sebastian, and we can share the load."

"Good idea!" said Sebastian.

CHAPTER THREE

Making a Plan

Since Sebastian's backpack was so heavy, the four of them left it on the floor in Wendy's house. Then she went to her closet to find her pink backpack while Wally and William went to their houses to find their backpacks.

Now they were all sitting on the floor of Wendy's house. They each had their own backpacks now and, of course, Wendy's was pink, Wally's was blue, and William's was purple.

The first thing they did was take everything out of Sebastian's gray backpack just to see what they had. Their plan was to divide things by weight, so that each one would be carrying about the same amount of weight.

"You really bought a lot of stuff," said Wendy.

"Yes," answered Sebastian. "The salesman at the camping and fishing shop showed me everything I needed to have a good and safe camping trip."

So the four of them divided everything that Sebastian had bought, and each friend put several things in their backpacks until the floor was empty.

"So far, so good," said William. "But we need to take a lot more than this if we're going on a camping trip."

"Like what?" asked Wally.

"Well, food, for one thing," answered William.

"You're right," said Wally. "We'll have to take enough food along to last the whole time. By the way, how long is this camping trip going to last?"

No one had thought of that yet.

Finally Wendy spoke: "You bring up a very good point, Wally. It's all well and good to have all the camping equipment we need. But we also need to do some planning."

"Good idea," said Sebastian. "So the first question, I think, should be: how long do we plan to go on our camping trip?"

"I think that depends on where we want to go," said Wendy.

"That's right," said William. "If we want to go to that high mountain, we have to figure out how long it will take us to get there and back again."

"What is the name of that mountain, by the way?" asked Sebastian.

"I don't know," answered Wendy. "We've lived here all our lives: someone should know."

Everyone was completely shocked when Wally said, "Mount Evergreen."

"What?" they all asked at the same time.

"Some of us do pay attention in school," said Wally with a big grin on his face.

"You know, I think he's right," said William. "I remember now that we learned about that mountain during our classes."

"Yes," added Sebastian. "And something else I just remembered: there are caves over there. They could be really fun to explore."

"Okay," said Wendy. "Now we agree where we want to go. Next we have to talk about how to get there."

"What do you mean?" asked Wally. "Don't we just start going in the direction of Mount Evergreen to get to Mount Evergreen?"

"Yes," answered Wendy. "But it's a little more than that. There will be things along the way that we need to know about."

"Like what?" asked Wally.

"Well, there might be some places that are really hard to go through," answered Wendy. "And right around the corner there might be an easier way."

"Yes," added William. "There might even be shortcuts to make it quicker to get there."

"Too bad we don't have a map," said Wally.

"Wally!" shouted Sebastian. "You're brilliant!"

This was not something that was heard every day, so Wendy and William waited patiently for Sebastian to explain why Wally was so brilliant.

"A map!" said Sebastian. "I completely forgot about the map."

"Which map?" asked Wendy.

Image: Dannyphoto80 | Dreamstime.com

"When I was at the camping and fishing shop, they sold me a map," answered Sebastian.

"So where is it?" asked William.

"I tucked it into one of the pockets of my new backpack," he answered. "We emptied it of all the bigger, heavier things, but we didn't check the pockets."

"Then I guess it's time to check the pockets," said Wendy.

Sebastian reached his hand in each pocket of the backpack: one pocket; another pocket; another pocket. Soon he had finished checking the inside of each pocket. He found a few other smaller things, but no map!

"I don't understand what happened," said Sebastian. "We've emptied the backpack, and now I've checked all the pockets. The backpack it completely empty now, and there's no map."

"Did you come here to my house directly from the camping and fishing shop?" asked Wendy.

Sebastian thought for a moment.

"No," he said.

"Where did you stop between the shop and here?" asked Wendy.

"I stopped at my house to take a little rest and have a little water because it had been quite a big job to get all this stuff from the shop to my house," answered Sebastian.

Wendy was quite smart. "When you got to your house, did you leave the backpack on your back, or did you put it down somewhere while you rested and drank your water?"

"Oh," answered Sebastian. "Now I remember what I did. The backpack was so heavy and I didn't know how to get it off. So I backed up against my kitchen table, and then the weight of the backpack was on the table instead of my shoulders. Then I slipped my arms out and the backpack stayed on top of the table."

Wendy thought for a second and then said, "This is just a guess, but I'm wondering if the map fell out of the backpack and slipped onto the table or maybe onto the floor or maybe under your table."

"That could be what happened," said Sebastian. "Especially if the map slipped under my table. Later, when I picked up the backpack, my back would have been to the table again, and maybe I didn't see it."

So while Wendy and Wally and William waited in Wendy's house, Sebastian left and went down to his house.

Would he find the map under his kitchen table?

CHAPTER FOUR

The Map

Sebastian rushed down to his house. He opened the door and ran towards his kitchen table looking for the map.

Where was it? Where was it?

He looked on top of the table; he looked under the table; he looked on the seats of the chairs that were pushed under the table; he looked on the floor all around the kitchen table. He even looked under the refrigerator: he thought it might have slipped under there.

There was no map in Sebastian's house.

He left and closed his door. He went back up to Wendy's house. Sebastian didn't need to say anything when he went inside Wendy's house. They could all tell by the expression on his face that he had not found the map.

"Well, we'll just have to go back to the shop and buy another map," said Wendy.

"We can't," said Sebastian.

"Why not?" asked William.

Wally was not a part of this conversation because he was too busy looking at the new camping equipment in each of the friends' backpacks.

"Because that was the last map in the shop," answered Sebastian. "I bought the last one."

"Now what will we do?" asked William.

Just then there was a knock on Wendy's front door.

"I wonder who that could be," she said.

It was Cherry the Chipmunk. Cherry was a very nice brown chipmunk who was known for being happy and cheery. Some people were not sure whether they should call her "Cherry the Chipmunk" or "Cheery the Chipmunk." Or maybe even "Cherry the Cheery Chipmunk.

But the best part was that she was holding a map!

"Did anyone lose this map?" she asked the group of friends.

"We did!" answered Sebastian.

"Where did you find it?" asked Wendy.

"It was on the floor of the forest just under your tree," answered Cherry. "You know: where everyone rests on the soft pine needles."

"That's brilliant!" said William. "Now we have our map."

"What kind of map is this?" asked Cherry.

"It is a map of this area," answered Sebastian. "It shows our tree, the rivers, the beaver lake, and other nearby areas, like the valleys and Mount Evergreen. That's where we're going on a camping trip."

"Wow!" said Cherry. "That sounds like fun."

"Do you want to go along?" asked Wendy.

"I'd love to," answered Cherry.

"Do you have a backpack?" asked Sebastian.

"I sure do," answered Cherry. Her backpack was brown because her favourite colour was brown and her coat of fur was mostly brown.

"When are you going to leave?" asked Cherry.

"As soon as we can figure out the best way to get to Mount Evergreen," answered Sebastian.

"I'll go and get my backpack and be back here as soon as I can," said Cherry.

"Don't forget to pack some food and water, okay?" asked Wendy.

"Okay," answered Cherry and she was out the door in a flash.

She didn't live very far away so it didn't take her long. In the meantime, the four friends spread the map on Wendy's kitchen table after she had cleared everything off of the top of the table.

They started to look at it when there was a knock at the door. It was Cherry.

"That was fast," said William.

"Do you mind helping to carry some of the camping equipment I bought this morning at the camping and fishing shop?" asked Sebastian.

"I don't mind at all," answered Cherry. "The more of us who are helping to carry things makes it so that it's not too heavy for one person."

She put her backpack down on the floor with the other backpacks and Sebastian put some of the camping equipment in her backpack. Then they went back to studying the map.

"So here we are at the old pine tree," said Wendy as she pointed at it on the map.

"And here's Mount Evergreen," said Sebastian as he pointed at the map.

"It looks like the most direct way is over Ridley's Ridge," said William.

"That might look like the most direct way, but you'll never make it," said Wally.

Because he had been quiet looking at the various pieces of camping equipment, everyone had forgotten about Wally!

"Why not?" asked Wendy.

"It is a very rocky ridge," he answered. "You'll never make it."

"How do you know these things?" asked Sebastian.

"Doesn't anyone pay attention in class?" asked Wally. "There is a steep cliff that no one can climb unless you are a professional rock climber."

"Okay," said Sebastian. "We'll have to go through this pass to the west of Ridley's Ridge."

"That'll work," said Wally as he went back to looking at the camping equipment.

"It's a little out of the way," said Wendy. "But I think we all agree that we want this trip to be a nice pleasant walk: nothing too difficult."

They all agreed. Plus it was summertime and it was hot, so they wanted to make the path as easy as possible.

The next problem they saw on the map was Raging River. It was a narrow river, but it was very dangerous because it moved very swiftly, and it was easy to get pulled down into the river.

"Does anybody have an idea how to cross this river?" asked William.

"I just had an idea," said Wendy. "This is a great map, but it doesn't show everything."

"What do you mean?" asked Sebastian.

"There might be a tree that has fallen across the river," answered Wendy.

"Or maybe there's a place where there are stepping stones," added Cherry.

"If we can cross Raging River then we will come to Runyon Ridge," said Sebastian.

"I wonder if it's rocky like Ridley Ridge?" asked William. "Wally, what do you remember about Runyon Ridge?"

"That one is easy," answered Wally.

"Why is that?" asked William.

"There is a cave that's like a tunnel," answered Wally. "It takes you to the valley where you start to climb up Mount Evergreen."

Perfect!

CHAPTER FIVE

Ready, Set, Go!

The great summertime camping adventure was about to begin. They were all still in Wendy's house making plans: Wendy, Wally, William, Sebastian, and Cherry.

They looked closely at their backpacks and what was in each one. They wanted to make sure that they had enough of everything for their trip, but they didn't want to take anything extra, or anything that they would not need. That would make their backpacks too heavy.

Now they were sure that they had everything ready for their big trip, including their map. So they said goodbye to each other for the night and left Wendy's house. They had decided to meet at the foot of the old pine tree early the next morning, just as the sun was beginning to rise.

Everyone was excited, but they all slept well. Cherry was the first to arrive at the foot of the tree because she had to travel a short distance to get to the old pine tree from her house and she had left her house a little extra early. One by one they joined Cherry. They were all very excited about their trip.

Soon they had all gathered with their backpacks at the foot of the tree, ready for the adventure to begin.

All except Wally!

"Where's Wally?" asked Wendy. "He should be down here and ready to go by now."

"I'll go and check on him," said William. William went back up the tree and knocked on Wally's door. There was no answer. Hmm, thought William, that's strange. He knocked again, but there was still no answer. He gently pushed on the door and it slowly opened.

"Wally!" said William. "Wally! It's me, William. We're ready to go."

William waited a little and then said, "Wally: it's time to get started."

There was still no answer so William opened Wally's bedroom door. And there he was, sound asleep.

"Wally!" yelled William. "It's time to go!"

Wally finally woke up. It was a good thing that his backpack was all ready to go.

Now they were all gathered at the foot of the old pine tree. They were excited and ready to get started.

Sebastian held the map since he had bought it. And Wendy walked next to him, since everyone knew how smart she was. After the two of these came William and Cherry. Wally was at the end of the group: he was constantly stopping and looking at things.

This was good in one way: it was a way for him to learn about things. But it was not good in another way, because the other four in the group did not want him to get too far behind them so that he got separated from them. So they often had to yell at him to keep up with them.

They walked away from the old pine tree and began walking through the forest in the direction of Ridley Ridge. They walked along Big River for a while: this was the river where the beavers had built a dam in the spring. Because it was such a big dam, it flooded a big area of the forest.

After the wife of the mean chief beaver chased him through the forest, there was a new chief beaver. He made the beaver lake smaller so that the flooded area of the forest was much smaller.

Today, as the five friends walked along Big River, they noticed it wasn't so big this year. It had been a dry summer without very much rain, so the river wasn't as big as it had been during other summers.

After walking along Big River for a while, their path took them away from the river.

The river curved to the left and their path continued straight ahead.

They walked over some small hills and across some small valleys. It was a nice summer day and it was not too hot, so they enjoyed the walk and talking with each other.

Soon they noticed that they were walking along the front of a hill. The hill was quite rocky and got higher and higher the further they walked. Now they knew where they were: they looked at the map to check. They were right: it was Ridley's Ridge.

And Wally had been spot on. This ridge was quite high and covered in huge rocks. There was no way to go directly over the ridge, so they had to keep walking along the front of it until it became less rocky and not quite so high and steep.

Ridley's Ridge was known to be a dangerous place because sometimes one of the rocks would become loose. Then it would come crashing down the hill. If you were walking along the foot of the ridge and a rock came crashing down towards you, you had better be fast at getting out of the way.

As they were walking in front of the most dangerous part of the ridge, they noticed a group of birds sitting at the top of the ridge. Everyone knew what they were: they were vultures!

This was a well-known place for vultures to gather and wait. Just one rock rolling down the side of Ridley's Ridge, and the vultures got out their white napkins to enjoy a meal.

Sebastian and Wendy were still walking in front with William and Cherry not too far behind. They kept looking around for Wally. They could see him, but he was walking so slowly that by now they could hardly see him any more.

Finally they stopped and turned back towards Wally and all shouted at him to try to keep up with them. Just then one of the biggest rocks came loose. It came crashing down the side of the ridge and landed with a huge noise right on the path behind the group of four.

But where was Wally?

The vultures licked their lips and put on their white napkins. They took off from where they had been sitting and swooped down towards the fallen rock.

CHAPTER SIX

Escape from Ridley's Ridge

The four friends quickly put their backpacks down on the path in front of Ridley's Ridge and began to run back in the direction where the rock had crashed. The vultures were quite big compared to the four other animals; the vultures were also scary looking and hungry looking too!

As they ran towards the rock in the path, they were all yelling, "Wally! Wally!" But there was no answer. And the vultures continued to swoop lower and lower towards the rock and the small animals.

As the four friends got closer to the fallen rock they could see what had happened. The big rock had landed between two other rocks on the path. There was a rock on the left side of the path and a rock on the right side of the path. And now there was a third rock jammed in between the two other rocks. This meant that the path was blocked.

"Now what should we do?" asked William.

"We'll have to go out around the rocks so that we can get back on the path but on the other side of the fallen rock," answered Wendy.

"But which way?" asked Sebastian. "To the right or to the left."

"I think we should go to the left," answered Wendy. "The rocks on the right are part of the ridge and they are very big and steep."

"You're right," said Cherry. "The rocks on the left look easier to climb over."

"And if we come to one that is too big, we can go out around it further to the left," added William.

So they began their search for Wally.

They climbed and walked and climbed and slid and climbed and finally they were back on the path again, on the side where they were sure they would be able to find Wally.

"Wally! Wally!" they all cried. But there was no answer.

"The last time we looked back at him, how far away was he?" asked Wendy.

"I didn't think he was too far behind us," answered Sebastian.

"You're right," added William. "I think he was getting tired of us yelling at him, so I think he had tried to catch up to us."

"You don't think…" started Cherry.

"What?" asked Wendy.

"You don't think… the big rock…" said Cherry.

"You think he was hit by that rock?" asked Wendy.

Everyone got quiet, because for the first time they began to think that Wally was no longer walking on the path, but was maybe under the big rock!

As they were quiet, they heard someone make a very tiny noise.

"Where is that coming from?" asked Wendy.

They were all facing away from the fallen rock, because they were so sure Wally was still far behind and on the path.

"I can't tell," answered William.

"Me neither," added Cherry.

Suddenly Sebastian gasped: "It's coming from the fallen rock!"

The vultures were flying lower and lower. They would reach the fallen rock at any moment.

"Quick!" yelled Wendy. "Run as fast as you can!"

The four friends ran along the path towards the fallen rock. They couldn't believe what they saw.

It was Wally. He was still alive, but he was under the rock. How was this possible? It was because the rock on the left side of the path and the rock on the right side of the path prevented the fallen rock from hitting the path.

Wally was on the path under the fallen rock, but he was still alive. The problem

was: he couldn't move!

"Are you okay, Wally?" asked Wendy.

"I guess," Wally answered in a weak voice. "This giant rock is on top of me, but not its entire weight. It just has me stuck here and I can't move."

"You just hold on and be patient and don't worry, Wally," said Wendy. "We'll come up with an idea on how to get you out of this situation."

They thought and they thought and they thought. But all they could think about was how heavy that rock was, and how impossible it would be to move it.

In the meantime, the vultures had landed nearby and were patiently waiting for their dinner.

"That rock must weigh a ton," said Sebastian.

"There's no way we can move it," said William.

"It's just too heavy for us to move it," added Cherry.

Suddenly Wendy let out a scream: "I've got it. We don't have to move the rock!"

"What are you talking about?" asked Sebastian. "Of course we have to move the rock."

"Are you a bird or a squirrel?" Wendy asked Sebastian.

"You know very well that I'm a squirrel," answered Sebastian.

"And what are squirrels good at?" asked Wendy.

Sebastian was confused. Suddenly he got it: "Digging holes."

So that was the plan.

Sebastian got as far under the fallen rock as he could and started to dig close to Wally. Then he moved to the right and continued to dig. Then he moved a little to the left and continued to dig.

He kept digging and each time the hole got just a little deeper. And suddenly Wally could move. They gently pulled him up out of the hole under the fallen rock.

"Wow!" said Wally. "Thank you so much. I was really scared under that rock."

By now the vultures had put away their white napkins and had flown back up to the top of the ridge: there was going to be no dinner tonight for the vultures!

The five friends now had to leave the fallen rock and the path. They had to go back around the lower set of rocks so they could get back to the path on the other side of the fallen rock. And now they came to the place where they had left their backpacks. It was hard work, but they finally made it. They picked up their backpacks and continued walking along the front of Ridley's Ridge on their way to Mount Evergreen.

CHAPTER SEVEN

Raging River

After their adventure at Ridley Rock, the five friends sat down along the path for some much needed rest and a snack.

"We forgot our white napkins," joked William. "Maybe the vultures will lend us their napkins."

They were now past Ridley Rock and getting close to Raging River. After their rest and snack, they packed up their backpacks and started walking on the path. Sebastian and Wendy were still acting as leaders.

After walking for a while, Wendy said, "What is that loud noise?"

No one knew, but as they continued to walk, the noise got louder and louder: it was Raging River.

When they finally saw it for the first time, they couldn't believe it. Whoever named it certainly gave it the right name. The water moved so quickly and the current was so strong, that no one would dare to try to cross it.

As they stood next to the river, they looked to the left and to the right. They didn't see any fallen trees that would act as a bridge.

"I think we should split up," said Wendy. "Some of us can walk to the left and some to the right and we'll be able to see if there's a fallen tree or rocks or some way to get across the river."

They all thought that was a good idea, so Wendy and William walked to the left while Sebastian and Cherry walked to the right. Wally stayed with all the backpacks.

Wendy and William walked for quite a long distance. They found some fallen trees, but none of these trees were long enough to stretch the whole way across the river to form a bridge. They came to a couple of places where there were some big rocks in the river, but the rocks were not close enough to each other to form stepping stones across the river.

Sebastian and Cherry found much the same things: short trees and rocks that didn't quite form stepping stones.

They walked back to where Wally was waiting, and shortly after that Wendy and William also returned.

They all reported to each other what they had seen.

"This is a difficult situation," said Wendy.

"There's no way to get across it," agreed Sebastian.

"It seems that way, doesn't it," said William.

"Maybe if we all close our eyes and think, an idea will come," said Cherry.

They all closed they eyes, even Wally, and tried to think of a way to get across Raging River. It sure made a lot of noise, but it didn't cover up every noise. At a nearby tree they heard a woodpecker.

Suddenly Wendy said, "That's it!"

"What?" asked Sebastian.

"William," said Wendy. "If we find a tree that's near the river and that's tall and not too thick, can you peck holes near the bottom of the tree like you're cutting it, and then we can push it so it falls across the river?"

"I sure can try," answered William. "We just have to find the right kind of tree. Like you said, it has to be close to the river bank; it can't be too thick; and it has to be tall enough to go the whole way across the river. Let's start looking!"

So they all walked along the bank of the Raging River, some to the left and some to the right.

"We've got one," shouted Sebastian. He and Cherry had found a tree just next to the bank of the river and it was tall and not too thick.

William and Wendy and Wally all ran to see what they had found. William said, "Yes, you're right: I think this will be perfect."

So he started pecking a hole, and then another and another until he had pecked holes the whole way around the bottom of the tree.

"Now all we have to do is push it in the right direction," said William.

They all got behind the tree and started to push. But it wasn't quite ready. So William had to peck a few more holes and then it was ready. They all pushed and the tree went the whole way across the river making a narrow but perfect bridge.

Sebastian said, "This could be dangerous, if someone slipped on the way over. I have an idea: let's each make two narrow poles. That way as we cross the river on the tree we'll each have two sticks to help us keep our balance if we lose our footing."

"Excellent idea," said William.

So they looked around near the river and each found two long narrow poles. They put on their backpacks, grabbed their poles and were ready to start their walk across Raging River.

Sebastian went first. They decided to go one at a time because the tree was narrow and they didn't want to put too much weight on it and make it sag. He held his two poles, one in each hand, and slowly made his way across the tree to the other side.

Wendy was next in line; then William; then Cherry; and finally Wally. Everything went fine until the end.

Wally was half way across the tree when he lost his footing and he dropped one of his two poles. He was swaying back and forth because he had lost his balance.

The good news was that, after he had reached the other side, Sebastian had taken off his backpack for two reasons. One, he was getting tired of carrying it; and two, he wanted to be free to help anyone who might have a problem or accident.

So Sebastian scampered out across the tree to help Wally.

"Hold on to your pole with your left hand," said Sebastian to Wally. "Now drop your backpack: I'll catch it."

Wally did as he was told. Now he had gotten back his balance and was safe. Sebastian carried Wally's backpack to the other side of the river and Wally followed.

They had all made it across Raging River!

CHAPTER EIGHT

The Cave

The five friends sat down for a little rest after the excitement of crossing the river. They opened their backpacks and pulled out some food. They all sat together in a circle and shared with each other the food they had brought with them in their backpacks.

"I was really scared," said Cherry.

"Me too," said Wally.

After they had rested for a while and had finished their meal, they started to put things back into their backpacks. Then they put on their backpacks and got ready to continue their adventure.

They had now gone around Ridley Ridge and had crossed Raging River. This river was in a valley between Ridley Ridge and the next ridge, Runyon Ridge. So now the five friends had to walk away from the river towards their next goal: Runyon Ridge and the cave that Wally had told them about.

They began to walk away from the river. The further away from the river they walked, the quieter the forest became. In some places in this valley there were trees, but as they continued to walk, they came out of the forest and found themselves in a large area of grassland and wildflowers.

"Wow!" said Sebastian. "Look at all of the pretty flowers!"

This was a meadow that was well-known to the deer that lived in the area. They often came here to find things to eat.

"Look over there," said William.

On the other side of the meadow far from where they stood, the five friends watched as a group of deer came out of the forest and began to eat. The deer saw the five friends, but they were not afraid of the five small animals walking on the path so far across the meadow.

After they had crossed the meadow and had said goodbye to the beautiful wildflowers, they entered the forest again. This forest was much like the other forests in the area, with rocks, trees, ferns, shrubs, and other plants.

As they continued to walk along the path, they began to notice that the area to the left side of the path was starting to get a little higher than the path and the right side of the path.

"I think this might be the beginning of Runyon Ridge," said Sebastian.

"I think you're right," said Wendy. "Let's have a quick look at your map."

Sebastian was carrying it folded, so they stopped and he unfolded the map.

"Here's Raging River," said Sebastian as they all looked over his shoulders at the map.

"And this looks like the meadow we just walked through," said Cherry.

"And here's Runyon Ridge," said Sebastian. He pointed at a spot on the map: "I think we're right about here."

He folded up the map but didn't put it away: he carried it so that he could open it quickly if he needed to.

So now they were were walking along the one side of Runyon Ridge.

"Wally," said Sebastian.

Wally wasn't listening as usual. After Sebastian had folded up the map, Wally had found a little salamander on a rock close to where the five friends had stopped.

"Wally," said Sebastian once more.

"Yes?" answered Wally. He had lost interest in the salamander mostly because it ran away when he had tried to touch it!

"What else do you know about this cave?" asked Sebastian.

"What cave?" asked Wally.

"The one you told us was like a tunnel that would take us over to the next valley before we reach the foot of Mount Evergreen," answered Wendy.

"Oh, yes, that's right," said Wally. "There is a cave that leads from one side of Runyon Ridge to the other side."

Wendy patiently said, "Yes, you had told us about the cave. But do you know anything else about it?"

"No," answered Wally. "That's all I know about it."

"The problem is that the cave is not marked on map," said Sebastian.

"You're sure there's a cave?" asked Wendy.

"I'm one hundred percent sure," answered Wally.

"Okay," said Sebastian. "We'll just have to keep walking and looking for the cave."

They continued down the path. Now they could see that Runyon Ridge was quite high, much higher than Ridley Ridge. And just as steep and rocky.

"It's a good thing there's a cave to get us to the next valley," said William. "These rocks are huge and the top of the ridge is so high."

After they had walked further down the path, they saw a fairly large opening in between two big rocks. It was the cave!

"This must be it," said Sebastian.

"It's quite wide for a tunnel, isn't it," said Wendy.

They stood at the entrance to the cave and looked into the darkness.

"You're right," said William. "It is wide, but it must be the cave that leads under the ridge over to the next valley."

Wendy still wasn't sure, but everyone wanted to get to the next valley, so they got out their torches and entered the cave.

They hadn't gone very far when they heard something.

"What is that noise?" asked Cherry.

"I don't know," answered Sebastian.

They walked a little further and there they saw what was making the noise.

"Oh look," said Cherry. "There are two little bear cubs playing."

"They are so cute," said Wally.

Wendy wasn't looking at the bear cubs: she was looking at the inside of the cave.

"Does anyone notice anything strange about this cave?" she asked the others.

"No," answered Sebastian. "Why?"

"Look around you," answered Wendy. "This is not a tunnel: this is the back of the cave and there is only the front entrance."

"You're right," said William. "This is just the home of the bear cubs."

"And where there are bear cubs there has to be a mother bear," said Wendy.

Just then they heard the scariest noise they had ever heard: it was the growl of a mother bear coming back to her den and finding a group of strangers close to her cubs!

CHAPTER NINE

The Second Cave

The five friends were so scared that they were shaking. The mother bear was standing at the entrance to the cave. She growled again and started to move towards the five animals that were standing between her and her two little cubs.

"What can we do?" asked William.

"I don't know," answered Sebastian.

"Do you think we can talk to her?" asked Cherry.

The mother bear growled even louder as she slowly walked closer to the five friends.

"I don't think so," answered Wendy.

Now the mother bear stood up on her two back legs and growled louder than ever.

"Quick," said Wendy. "Everybody take some food out of your backpacks and put it on top of that rock over there."

They all did what she had suggested. Suddenly the bear got down on all fours and walked towards the food. She was more interested in what was on top of the rock than the five friends.

"Run!" shouted Sebastian.

They all grabbed their backpacks and ran out of the cave. They continued running down the path and when they looked around, they saw the mother bear at the entrance to her den. She was growling at them again, but she was staying with her two cubs.

After they reached a safe distance, the five friend stopped to rest.

"Wow!" said Wally. "That was close!"

"I don't think I've ever been so scared in my life," said Cherry.

They all agreed. After resting for a while, they grabbed their backpacks and began to walk again. Soon they came to another cave.

"Do you think this is the right one?" asked William.

"Well it isn't big and wide like the bear's den," answered Sebastian.

"We'll just have to give it a try and see what we find," added Wendy.

So the five friends got their torches out of their backpacks and got ready to enter the cave. They were a little scared because of what happened inside the last cave, but they continued on.

"I think this might be it," said Sebastian.

"I agree," said William. "It's more like a tunnel."

It was long and narrow and not very high. Suddenly they heard some noises.

"What was that?" asked Cherry.

No one knew until Wendy finally said, "Look up there!" She pointed her torch at the ceiling.

Hanging from the ceiling of the cave were lots of tiny bats. Most of them were hanging upside down and sleeping, while some of them were flying around looking for a good place to hang.

After the scary time with the mother bear, the five friends were glad that there were only bats in this cave. So far, so good, but no one knew what was ahead of them in this long tunnel.

Suddenly Sebastian shouted, "Look!"

Everyone was scared because they thought he had seen a dangerous animal. But he was pointing at some strange looking worms that were hanging down from the top of the ceiling.

"What are they?" asked Cherry.

"Switch off your torches," said Wendy. She knew what they were.

They were glowworms. There were many of them all together in one area, so it was almost like having a ceiling light in the room of a house. The light from all of the glowworms brightened a big area of the tunnel.

The five friends stood for a while so that they could enjoy this special show that

Image: © Patchanu Noree | Dreamstime.com

nature was giving them. And then they switched their torches back on and continued through the tunnel.

They came to a very wide and high open area. It was beautiful.

"I always forget which are stalactites and which are stalagmites," said William.

"I learned a way to remember that," said Wally. "The word 'stalactite' has the letter 'C' in it and the word 'ceiling' has the letter 'C' in it. So stalactites hang down from the ceiling of a cave and stalagmites do not."

"That's a great way to remember it," said William.

Wendy wasn't saying very much, and Cherry noticed it.

"Are you not enjoying the stalactites and the stalagmites, Wendy?" asked Cherry.

"Yes, they are beautiful," answered Wendy. "It's just that I'm a little worried that we have the wrong cave again. Is this the end of the cave or does it continue?"

They all walked around the large area of the cave and used their torches to try to find a place where the tunnel continued.

Suddenly Sebastian had an idea. "Let's switch off our torches and see if we notice any light."

"Good idea," said Wendy. "And we can also stand still and feel if there is a little breeze going through the cave."

The five friends all switched off their torches and stood still in the darkness. They stood there for a long time, but no one noticed anything.

Suddenly Wendy said, "There it is!"

There was an opening that was hidden because of a large stalagmite standing in front of it.

"Three cheers for Wendy," said Sebastian.

They had not yet reached the next valley, but at least they had hope that this was not a dead-end cave, and that it was the tunnel that Wally had told them about.

They gathered their backpacks and torches and walked around the big stalagmite. The tunnel became smaller and smaller. They were all starting to think that this was the end of the cave when Sebastian suddenly yelled, "Switch off your torches."

They all did as he said.

"Look ahead," he said.

"I can't see anything," said Wendy.

"Wait until you eyes get used to the darkness," said Sebastian.

She and the others waited a little while and suddenly Wendy shouted, "I see it. It's light. It's the light at the end of the tunnel!"

The others could see it too. They continued towards the light and it got brighter and brighter. Now they came to the exit of the tunnel and looked around them.

They were in the valley on the other side of Runyon Ridge, but what was more important was that they were standing at the foot of Mount Evergreen!

CHAPTER TEN

Mount Evergreen!

The five friends walked away from the tunnel and followed the path in front of them. It was an easy path to follow because so many people used it: Mount Evergreen was a very popular place to hike.

The path did not go straight up the mountain: it was a little too steep for that. Instead it zigzagged back and forth to make it easier for the adventurers.

"What a beautiful day to climb this mountain," said Cherry.

"Yes," agreed Sebastian. "And at this time of day it's not quite so hot."

It was now late in the afternoon and the sun was slowly moving west.

"Let's hope there will still be daylight when we reach the top so that we can set up our tent," said William.

"We should be okay," said Sebastian. "I don't think it's going to take us very long to reach the top."

The five friends continued to follow the path. They passed a beautiful waterfall. They stopped here for a short time just to dip their feet in the pool at the bottom of the waterfall. There were ferns and mossy rocks around the pool: it was one of the most beautiful places they had seen on their trip so far.

After the waterfall, they continued on their way up the mountain. The path started to get a little steeper as they climbed higher. Finally the path opened up into a large flat area. They stopped and looked behind them.

"Wow!" they all said together.

The view from the top of Mount Evergreen was amazing. They could see where they had come from.

"Look down at the foot of the mountain," said William. "There's the tunnel and Runyon Ridge."

They looked on the other side of the ridge. "There's the meadow with the wildflowers and the deer," said Cherry.

And beyond that they could see more. "Can you see Raging River?" asked Wendy. "It's just beyond that area of forest."

"And look beyond that," said Wally. "There's Ridley Ridge. I think I can even see the rock I was stuck under. And the vultures. And their white napkins."

He was joking, of course, and they all laughed.

Then suddenly Wendy said, "Look! Can you see it? It's the old pine tree."

And there it was, far off in the distance, but because it was so tall, they could still see it.

After they had enjoyed the view for a while, Sebastian said, "We should probably set up the tent and get our campsite ready before the sun goes down."

Everyone helped. They laid out the tent and set up a pole inside in the middle of the tent. They all got out their sleeping bags and put them side by side inside the tent.

"Now that that is finished, we can think about building a campfire," said William.

They all gathered leaves and sticks and twigs and a couple of logs. They used rocks to make a circle on the ground in front of their tent. This was for their campfire.

After making the campfire and having something to eat, Wendy said, "I don't know about the rest of you, but I'm really tired after that long trip. I'm going to bed."

"Me too," said William. One by one they agreed it was time to get some sleep.

They put out the campfire because they didn't want it to burn during the night while they were sleeping. They all got into their sleeping bags, said goodnight, and fell asleep.

The next morning when they woke up, the sun was just starting to peek through the forest down below. They rolled up their sleeping bags and took down the tent. They ate the food that was left over and soon they were ready for their return journey.

Just before they left, they stopped one more time to look at the views all around them. There were views not just of the places they had been, but there so many other places they could see from the top of Mount Evergreen.

"Look over there," said Wendy. "There's a huge lake."

"And over there's another waterfall," said Sebastian.

"And another mountain that looks almost as big as Mount Evergreen," added Cherry.

It was hard for them to leave, because there was so much to see.

"It makes you think, doesn't it?" asked Wendy.

"What?" asked Wally.

"About the world, and how big it is and how many things there are to see and how many places there are to go," answered Wendy.

"It makes you want to see everyplace, doesn't it?" asked Sebastian.

"It does," answered William.

The five friends finally began their journey back home. Going down Mount Evergreen was much easier than going up!

They easily found the tunnel through Runyon Ridge and enjoyed the wildflowers again in the meadow.

They were able to find the same little bridge they had made to get across Raging River, so that was not a problem.

And they were able to get around Ridley Ridge without any falling rocks and no bothersome vultures with white napkins.

And now they just had to walk back home, through the forest and towards the old pine tree.

The old pine tree: it was always there waiting for them. No matter where they went on their adventures or how often they went away, the old pine tree was always there.

The End

Edward Alan Kurtz

Edward is an American writer.

He specializes in writing works of fiction and non-fiction for children, as well as travel books and articles.

Ed was born in Pennsylvania and completed several university degrees.

He lived for many years in Honolulu, Hawaii, and now lives and writes in Thailand.

Previous books:

- Max and The Map
- Christmas in the Forest
- Springtime in the Forest

~ • ~

www.ingramcontent.com/pod-product-compliance
Lightning Source LLC
Chambersburg PA
CBHW042036100526
44587CB00030B/4450